BLAZERS®

GROSS JOBS
Working with
ANIMALS

by Nikki Bruno

raintree
a Capstone company — publishers for children

Raintree is an imprint of Capstone Global Library Limited, a company incorporated in England and Wales having its registered office at 264 Banbury Road, Oxford, OX2 7DY – Registered company number: 6695582

www.raintree.co.uk
myorders@raintree.co.uk

Edited by Hank Musolf
Designed by Bobbie Nuytten
Original illustrations © Capstone Global Library Limited 2019
Picture research by Heather Mauldin
Production by Katy LaVigne
Originated by Capstone Global Library Ltd
Printed and bound in India

ISBN 978 1 4747 7507 6
22 21 20 19 18
10 9 8 7 6 5 4 3 2 1

British Library Cataloguing in Publication Data
A full catalogue record for this book is available from the British Library.

Acknowledgements
We would like to thank the following for permission to reproduce photographs:
Alamy: Astrid Hinderks, 26-27, Chris Howes/Wild Places, 20-21, Farlap, 19, Peter Horree, 22-23, robertharding, 8-9, Tim Brown, 4-5; ASSOCIATED PRESS: Brian Davies/The Register-Guard, 10-11; iStockphoto: fcafotodigital, 10 (inset), groveb, 14, M_a_y_a, 24-25, Morsa Images, 28-29, nechaev-kon, 24 (inset), Singkham, 20 (inset); Minden Pictures: Francois Savigny, 12-13, Kevin Schafer, 26 (inset), Pete Oxford, 12 (inset); Newscom: CHARLES BERTRAM/KRT, 15; Shutterstock: Alexey Savchuk, 16-17, cate_89, cover, 1, ESB Professional, 4 (inset), ShutterDivision, 6-7. Design Elements: Shutterstock: Alhovik, kasha_malasha, Katsiaryna Chumakova, Yellow Stocking.

Every effort has been made to contact copyright holders of material reproduced in this book. Any omissions will be rectified in subsequent printings if notice is given to the publisher.

All the internet addresses (URLs) given in this book were valid at the time of going to press. However, due to the dynamic nature of the internet, some addresses may have changed, or sites may have changed or ceased to exist since publication. While the author and publisher regret any inconvenience this may cause readers, no responsibility for any such changes can be accepted by either the author or the publisher.

CONTENTS

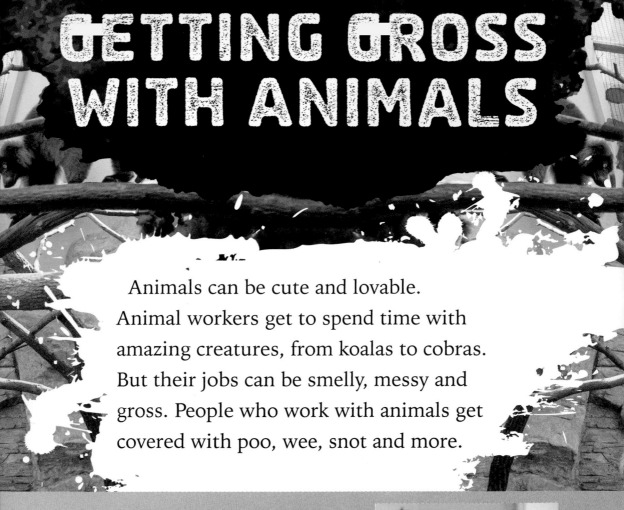

GETTING GROSS
WITH ANIMALS

Animals can be cute and lovable. Animal workers get to spend time with amazing creatures, from koalas to cobras. But their jobs can be smelly, messy and gross. People who work with animals get covered with poo, wee, snot and more.

DID YOU KNOW?

In the UK, 45 per cent of the population own a pet. Dogs are the most popular, with 26 per cent of people owning one.

VET TECH

Vet techs help vets. They check the animals' coats for fleas. They clean dirty teeth and treat **pus**-filled wounds. Vet techs also help with operations. They see and smell the insides of animals.

GROSS-O-METER

DID YOU KNOW?

Dogs have liquid-filled **glands** where their poo comes out. Vet techs may have to squeeze out the smelly liquid.

pus yellowish-white fluid found in sores and infections

gland organ in the body that makes certain chemicals

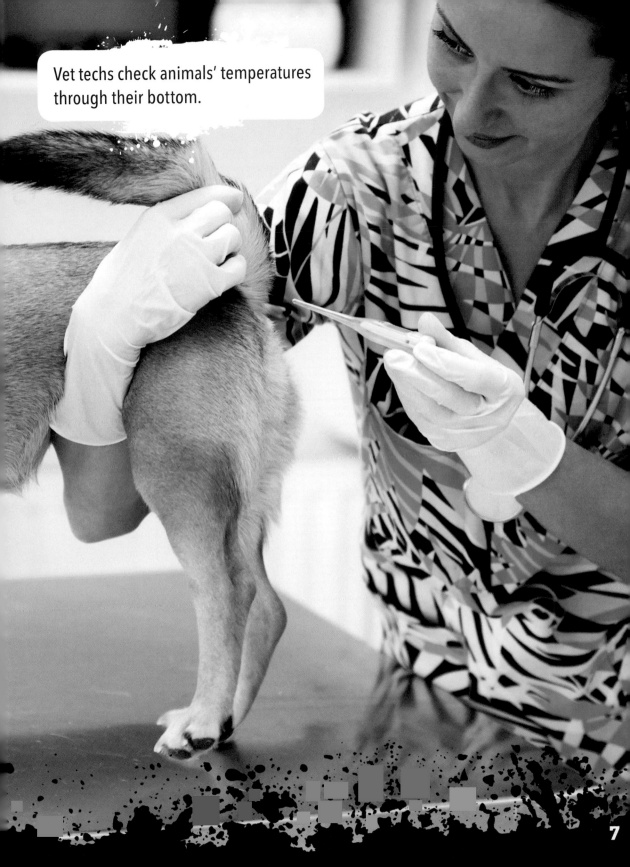

Vet techs check animals' temperatures through their bottom.

WHALE SNOT COLLECTOR

Scientists study whale snot to learn about them. Who collects this goo? Whale snot collectors do! They pick up the snot with a long pole. It's normal to get blasted by whale sneezes while getting the snot!

GROSS-O-METER

DID YOU KNOW?

Snot collection is so gross that some scientists make a **drone** do the dirty work. It is called a SnotBot.

drone unmanned, remote-controlled aircraft

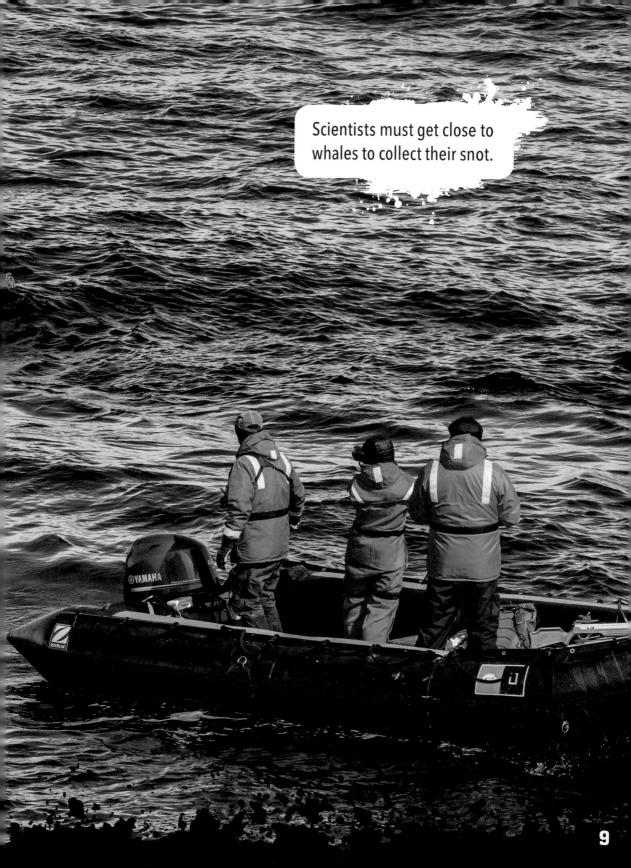

Scientists must get close to whales to collect their snot.

PEST CONTROLLER

Pest controllers remove pests from people's homes and businesses. They get up close to termites, rats, ants, bats and other animals. These workers use traps and dangerous poisons. Sometimes they have to carry the pests out by hand!

GROSS-O-METER

DID YOU KNOW?

Cockroaches breathe through holes in their body. A cockroach can live for a week without its head.

pest controller person who rids places of unwanted pests for a living

SNAKE RESEARCHER

What's grosser than a snake? Its vomit! Snake researchers look at snake vomit to find out what snakes eat. First, they squeeze the snake to make it throw up. Then they study the vomit.

GROSS-O-METER

DID YOU KNOW?

Snakes do not want to be caught! They often wee and poo on researchers.

Snakes don't poo as often as other animals.

DEER WEE FARMER

Who in the world would want to collect deer wee? These farmers do! Deer wee farmers lead deer to a building with floors that collect wee. The wee is stored in fridges. Deer hunters use the wee as **bait** to attract male deer.

GROSS-O-METER

DID YOU KNOW?

The number of deer in Michigan, USA, is unusually high. All of the deer wee is harming Michigan's hemlock trees.

bait something that attracts creatures so that they can be caught

MAGGOT FARMER

Maggots are disgusting! These squirmy, worm-like creatures are young flies. Maggot farmers **breed** and package millions of them. They sell maggots as fish bait and farm animal food.

FLESH EATERS

GROSS-O-METER

Maggots don't just look gross. They also eat gross food. Their favourites are dead animals. Flies lay their eggs on living or dead animals. After hatching, the maggots have a ready-made meal.

breed mate and raise a certain type of animal

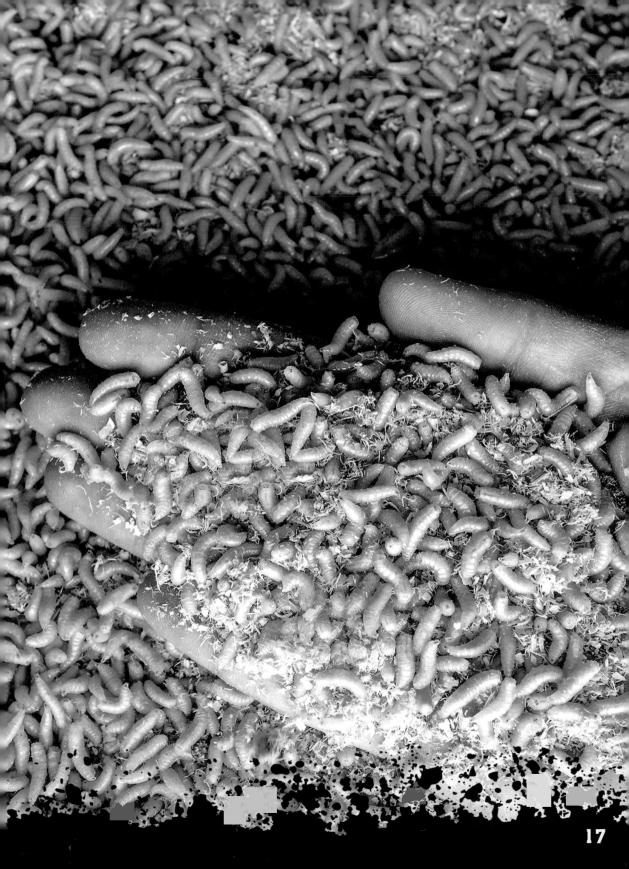

COW HOOF TRIMMER

Cow hoof trimming is a lot messier than clipping nails! Cows must be roped down on a special device. The trimmers use special tools to shave away the hooves. It's normal to get covered in cow poo in the process!

GROSS-O-METER

DID YOU KNOW?

Cow hoof trimmers don't just trim cows' hooves. They may treat sores. They may give care to cows that are having trouble walking.

GUANO COLLECTOR

Some people do their jobs knee-deep in bat poo. Others scrape bird poo off rocks. These workers are called **guano** collectors. Guano is a great **fertilizer**. It also keeps pests away from plants.

GROSS-O-METER

DID YOU KNOW?

In 1850 guano was worth one-quarter the price of gold. It was one of the best fertilizers at that time.

guano dried bird or bat droppings, used as fertilizer

fertilizer substance used to make crops grow better

Guano collectors often find bat poo in caves.

LEATHER TANNER

Leather is made in a messy process called tanning. First, tanners take the animals' skin off. Then they remove hair, blood and flesh. The skin gets soaked, scraped and sanded. Over time it becomes soft and flexible.

GROSS-O-METER

DID YOU KNOW?

Leather tanning has changed over time. Leather tanners used to use vegetables, smoke or even animal fat to turn animal skins into leather.

DOG GROOMER

Dog groomers deal with poo, wee, fleas, drool and dog breath. They clip nails, scrub dirt, pick off fleas and clean out ears. They also get covered in dog hair.

GROSS-O-METER

DID YOU KNOW?

Groomers need to be careful when cleaning pets with fleas or ticks. These gross creatures can move from the pet to the groomer!

tick

groom clean and make an animal look tidy

ZOOKEEPER

When hundreds of wild animals live in a small area, things get dirty fast! Zookeepers shovel elephant poo. They handle raw meat and smelly fish. Animals spit and wee on zookeepers. Monkeys might even throw poo at them.

DID YOU KNOW?

Most animals leave their poo where it drops. Sloths spend most of their time in trees. To poo, they slowly climb down the tree. They poo on the ground. Then they neatly bury their poo in the ground. Sloths poo once a week.

THANK YOU ANIMAL WORKERS!

What would the world be like without animal workers? They keep our pets healthy. They keep zoos clean. They get rid of pests. They brave a lot of gross things to get their jobs done!

GLOSSARY

bait something that attracts creatures so that they can be caught

breed mate and raise a certain type of animal

drone unmanned, remote-controlled aircraft

fertilizer substance used to make crops grow better

gland organ in the body that makes certain chemicals

groom clean and make an animal look tidy

guano dried bird or bat droppings, used as fertilizer

pest controller person who rids places of unwanted pests for a living

pus yellowish-white fluid found in sores and infections

FIND OUT MORE

BOOKS

Animals (Jobs If You Like...), Charlotte Guillain (Raintree, 2013)

Dog Walker (Diary of a...), Angela Royston (Raintree, 2014)

Who Scoops Elephant Poo? Working at a Zoo (Wild Work), Margie Markarian (Raintree, 2010)

WEBSITES

www.bbc.co.uk/cbbc/shows/pet-school
Follow these tips for looking after pets.

www.dkfindout.com/uk/animals-and-nature/anteaters-and-sloths/sloths
Find out more about sloths.

INDEX